HOMEMAKER'S FRIEND

2018 Daily PLANNER

Sue Hooley

The 2018 Homemaker's Friend Daily Planner
is dedicated to
MY DAUGHTER, SHARLA
Without our planner sessions, we'd succumb to chaos.

An imprint of Christian Light Publications

2018 DAILY PLANNER

Christian Light Publications, Inc.
Harrisonburg, Virginia 22802

13 Digit ISBN: 978-0-87813-263-8

To order planners by mail, please use order form in back.
Your comments and suggestions are welcomed!

Cover Design: Lanette Steiner
Text Design: Rhoda Miller & Lanette Steiner

A SPECIAL NOTE OF THANKS

to Katherine Derstine

for choosing the Scripture verses.

The verses contain the theme of PRAISE & GLADNESS.

HOLMES PRINTING SOLUTIONS

8757 County Road 77 . Fredericksburg, Ohio 44627 . 888.473.6870

THIS **DAILY PLANNER** BELONGS TO:

_____

_____

_____

_____

_____

IMPORTANT PHONE NUMBERS:

NAME

PHONE

TWO THOUSAND SEVENTEEN

JANUARY 17

S	M	T	W	T	F	S
1	2	3	4	5	6	7
8	9	10	11	12	13	14
15	16	17	18	19	20	21
22	23	24	25	26	27	28
29	30	31				

FEBRUARY 17

S	M	T	W	T	F	S
			1	2	3	4
5	6	7	8	9	10	11
12	13	14	15	16	17	18
19	20	21	22	23	24	25
26	27	28				

MARCH 17

S	M	T	W	T	F	S
			1	2	3	4
5	6	7	8	9	10	11
12	13	14	15	16	17	18
19	20	21	22	23	24	25
26	27	28	29	30	31	

APRIL 17

S	M	T	W	T	F	S
						1
2	3	4	5	6	7	8
9	10	11	12	13	14	15
16	17	18	19	20	21	22
23	24	25	26	27	28	29
30						

MAY 17

S	M	T	W	T	F	S
	1	2	3	4	5	6
7	8	9	10	11	12	13
14	15	16	17	18	19	20
21	22	23	24	25	26	27
28	29	30	31			

JUNE 17

S	M	T	W	T	F	S
				1	2	3
4	5	6	7	8	9	10
11	12	13	14	15	16	17
18	19	20	21	22	23	24
25	26	27	28	29	30	

JULY 17

S	M	T	W	T	F	S
						1
2	3	4	5	6	7	8
9	10	11	12	13	14	15
16	17	18	19	20	21	22
23	24	25	26	27	28	29
30	31					

AUGUST 17

S	M	T	W	T	F	S
		1	2	3	4	5
6	7	8	9	10	11	12
13	14	15	16	17	18	19
20	21	22	23	24	25	26
27	28	29	30	31		

SEPTEMBER 17

S	M	T	W	T	F	S
					1	2
3	4	5	6	7	8	9
10	11	12	13	14	15	16
17	18	19	20	21	22	23
24	25	26	27	28	29	30

OCTOBER 17

S	M	T	W	T	F	S
1	2	3	4	5	6	7
8	9	10	11	12	13	14
15	16	17	18	19	20	21
22	23	24	25	26	27	28
29	30	31				

NOVEMBER 17

S	M	T	W	T	F	S
			1	2	3	4
5	6	7	8	9	10	11
12	13	14	15	16	17	18
19	20	21	22	23	24	25
26	27	28	29	30		

DECEMBER 17

S	M	T	W	T	F	S
					1	2
3	4	5	6	7	8	9
10	11	12	13	14	15	16
17	18	19	20	21	22	23
24	25	26	27	28	29	30
31						

TWO THOUSAND EIGHTEEN

JANUARY 18

S	M	T	W	T	F	S
	1	2	3	4	5	6
7	8	9	10	11	12	13
14	15	16	17	18	19	20
21	22	23	24	25	26	27
28	29	30	31			

FEBRUARY 18

S	M	T	W	T	F	S
				1	2	3
4	5	6	7	8	9	10
11	12	13	14	15	16	17
18	19	20	21	22	23	24
25	26	27	28			

MARCH 18

S	M	T	W	T	F	S
				1	2	3
4	5	6	7	8	9	10
11	12	13	14	15	16	17
18	19	20	21	22	23	24
25	26	27	28	29	30	31

APRIL 18

S	M	T	W	T	F	S
1	2	3	4	5	6	7
8	9	10	11	12	13	14
15	16	17	18	19	20	21
22	23	24	25	26	27	28
29	30					

MAY 18

S	M	T	W	T	F	S
		1	2	3	4	5
6	7	8	9	10	11	12
13	14	15	16	17	18	19
20	21	22	23	24	25	26
27	28	29	30	31		

JUNE 18

S	M	T	W	T	F	S
					1	2
3	4	5	6	7	8	9
10	11	12	13	14	15	16
17	18	19	20	21	22	23
24	25	26	27	28	29	30

JULY 18

S	M	T	W	T	F	S
1	2	3	4	5	6	7
8	9	10	11	12	13	14
15	16	17	18	19	20	21
22	23	24	25	26	27	28
29	30	31				

AUGUST 18

S	M	T	W	T	F	S
			1	2	3	4
5	6	7	8	9	10	11
12	13	14	15	16	17	18
19	20	21	22	23	24	25
26	27	28	29	30	31	

SEPTEMBER 18

S	M	T	W	T	F	S
						1
2	3	4	5	6	7	8
9	10	11	12	13	14	15
16	17	18	19	20	21	22
23	24	25	26	27	28	29
30						

OCTOBER 18

S	M	T	W	T	F	S
	1	2	3	4	5	6
7	8	9	10	11	12	13
14	15	16	17	18	19	20
21	22	23	24	25	26	27
28	29	30	31			

NOVEMBER 18

S	M	T	W	T	F	S
				1	2	3
4	5	6	7	8	9	10
11	12	13	14	15	16	17
18	19	20	21	22	23	24
25	26	27	28	29	30	

DECEMBER 18

S	M	T	W	T	F	S
						1
2	3	4	5	6	7	8
9	10	11	12	13	14	15
16	17	18	19	20	21	22
23	24	25	26	27	28	29
30	31					

TWO THOUSAND NINETEEN

JANUARY 19

S	M	T	W	T	F	S
		1	2	3	4	5
6	7	8	9	10	11	12
13	14	15	16	17	18	19
20	21	22	23	24	25	26
27	28	29	30	31		

FEBRUARY 19

S	M	T	W	T	F	S
					1	2
3	4	5	6	7	8	9
10	11	12	13	14	15	16
17	18	19	20	21	22	23
24	25	26	27	28		

MARCH 19

S	M	T	W	T	F	S
					1	2
3	4	5	6	7	8	9
10	11	12	13	14	15	16
17	18	19	20	21	22	23
24	25	26	27	28	29	30
31						

APRIL 19

S	M	T	W	T	F	S
	1	2	3	4	5	6
7	8	9	10	11	12	13
14	15	16	17	18	19	20
21	22	23	24	25	26	27
28	29	30				

MAY 19

S	M	T	W	T	F	S
			1	2	3	4
5	6	7	8	9	10	11
12	13	14	15	16	17	18
19	20	21	22	23	24	25
26	27	28	29	30	31	

JUNE 19

S	M	T	W	T	F	S
						1
2	3	4	5	6	7	8
9	10	11	12	13	14	15
16	17	18	19	20	21	22
23	24	25	26	27	28	29
30						

JULY 19

S	M	T	W	T	F	S
	1	2	3	4	5	6
7	8	9	10	11	12	13
14	15	16	17	18	19	20
21	22	23	24	25	26	27
28	29	30	31			

AUGUST 19

S	M	T	W	T	F	S
				1	2	3
4	5	6	7	8	9	10
11	12	13	14	15	16	17
18	19	20	21	22	23	24
25	26	27	28	29	30	31

SEPTEMBER 19

S	M	T	W	T	F	S
1	2	3	4	5	6	7
8	9	10	11	12	13	14
15	16	17	18	19	20	21
22	23	24	25	26	27	28
29	30					

OCTOBER 19

S	M	T	W	T	F	S
		1	2	3	4	5
6	7	8	9	10	11	12
13	14	15	16	17	18	19
20	21	22	23	24	25	26
27	28	29	30	31		

NOVEMBER 19

S	M	T	W	T	F	S
					1	2
3	4	5	6	7	8	9
10	11	12	13	14	15	16
17	18	19	20	21	22	23
24	25	26	27	28	29	30

DECEMBER 19

S	M	T	W	T	F	S
1	2	3	4	5	6	7
8	9	10	11	12	13	14
15	16	17	18	19	20	21
22	23	24	25	26	27	28
29	30	31				

TWO THOUSAND TWENTY

JANUARY 20

S	M	T	W	T	F	S
			1	2	3	4
5	6	7	8	9	10	11
12	13	14	15	16	17	18
19	20	21	22	23	24	25
26	27	28	29	30	31	

FEBRUARY 20

S	M	T	W	T	F	S
						1
2	3	4	5	6	7	8
9	10	11	12	13	14	15
16	17	18	19	20	21	22
23	24	25	26	27	28	29

MARCH 20

S	M	T	W	T	F	S
1	2	3	4	5	6	7
8	9	10	11	12	13	14
15	16	17	18	19	20	21
22	23	24	25	26	27	28
29	30	31				

APRIL 20

S	M	T	W	T	F	S
			1	2	3	4
5	6	7	8	9	10	11
12	13	14	15	16	17	18
19	20	21	22	23	24	25
26	27	28	29	30		

MAY 20

S	M	T	W	T	F	S
					1	2
3	4	5	6	7	8	9
10	11	12	13	14	15	16
17	18	19	20	21	22	23
24	25	26	27	28	29	30
31						

JUNE 20

S	M	T	W	T	F	S
	1	2	3	4	5	6
7	8	9	10	11	12	13
14	15	16	17	18	19	20
21	22	23	24	25	26	27
28	29	30				

JULY 20

S	M	T	W	T	F	S
			1	2	3	4
5	6	7	8	9	10	11
12	13	14	15	16	17	18
19	20	21	22	23	24	25
26	27	28	29	30	31	

AUGUST 20

S	M	T	W	T	F	S
						1
2	3	4	5	6	7	8
9	10	11	12	13	14	15
16	17	18	19	20	21	22
23	24	25	26	27	28	29
30	31					

SEPTEMBER 20

S	M	T	W	T	F	S
		1	2	3	4	5
6	7	8	9	10	11	12
13	14	15	16	17	18	19
20	21	22	23	24	25	26
27	28	29	30			

OCTOBER 20

S	M	T	W	T	F	S
				1	2	3
4	5	6	7	8	9	10
11	12	13	14	15	16	17
18	19	20	21	22	23	24
25	26	27	28	29	30	31

NOVEMBER 20

S	M	T	W	T	F	S
1	2	3	4	5	6	7
8	9	10	11	12	13	14
15	16	17	18	19	20	21
22	23	24	25	26	27	28
29	30					

DECEMBER 20

S	M	T	W	T	F	S
		1	2	3	4	5
6	7	8	9	10	11	12
13	14	15	16	17	18	19
20	21	22	23	24	25	26
27	28	29	30	31		

REALISTIC IDEALISM

From my kitchen window, I could see a green plant by the edge of the harvested wheat field. Curious, I took a closer look and was surprised to see a sunflower. Not that a volunteer sunflower is usually so rare, but this beauty prospered in the hottest and driest summer on record in northeastern Washington. I was amazed at its perfection.

Sunflowers are drought-resistant, but according to research, they still need water especially in the weeks prior to blooming. There might be a scientific fact to explain how this sunflower bloomed without water, but perhaps God provided an allegory to encourage me to keep growing and blooming at a time when my days seemed less than ideal.

The dictionary gives two definitions for *ideal*:

1) Satisfying one's conception of what is perfect; most suitable.

2) Existing only in the imagination; desirable or perfect but not likely to become a reality.

Definition one happens regularly. For instance, a picnic may provide the relaxation we need during a hectic summer. We may say it was ideal, especially if the weather was pleasant and the bugs were few.

Definition two is the most likely to cause us trouble. We can form concepts and opinions on how daily life *should* happen. Thus we can rob ourselves of the ability to enjoy life the way it is.

I fight an ongoing battle between realism and idealism. For example, if I am planning a baby shower, I prefer cute homemade baby shower invitations over generic ones from the Dollar Store. Idealism says, "Do it. Making cards is creative, plus it is something you love to do." Reality says, "Don't do it. You have a toddler, and Aunt Mandy is coming for a visit the same week as the baby shower."

Striving for your ideals like keeping a cleaning schedule, completing laundry on wash day, and washing dishes after every meal are great aspirations. But sometimes life gets in the way. Maybe you need a nap before you finish the laundry or a sick child rearranges the cleaning plans. Ideals and goals are motivating, but sometimes we must consider other options to make the best choice *just for today*.

Perhaps we begin homemaking with a set of expectations about what it means to be an ideal homemaker. Those beliefs may come from our upbringings or through our perceived expectations of friends and family. Sometimes those ideals are based on real pressures, but many times they are strictly hypothetical.

How should we respond when daily life is not like we anticipated? If that little sunflower can grow and bloom in less-than-ideal circumstances, we probably can too. Here are five ways to let go of ideals.

LEARN TO FLOW. Have you, like I, wondered why we cannot calmly accept a change? These little inconveniences are usually short-term and only rearrange an hour or a day, so why do they seem like a big deal? Perhaps it's because our weary bodies and brains are ready for rest, and an unforeseen issue overloads our humanity. Other times it might simply be our selfish nature that wishes life to happen our way.

HAVE A MERRY HEART. Haven't we all felt the relief of tension from a good hearty laugh? Proverbs 17:22 says, "A merry heart doeth good like a medicine." Medical research concludes that laughter increases blood flow, boosts the immune system, and helps you relax. Stressful moments *will* happen, and laughter *will* lighten the moment. A grateful spirit will help put the negatives and positives of daily living into perspective.

LOOK FOR BLESSINGS. Have you noticed that the challenges we face often contain a blessing in disguise? It's hard to remember this when someone spills pickle juice on the floor, but it is an opportunity to exercise Christian graces. Many times less-than-ideal happenings that interrupt our schedules are God's way of accomplishing His plan for us.

STREAMLINE YOUR DAYS. Make sure your schedule is not too full. Juggling a dozen activities doesn't make you a better person; it can add stress and take joy out of living. Simplify. Fewer toys and simpler meals can make your days more manageable. Sometimes a quick fix is better than no fix at all. As far as I know, an occasional swish of dirt under the rug has never hurt anybody.

LET GOD HANDLE IT. Sometimes it is difficult to distinguish the difference between the ideal and doing what is currently best for your situation. God gives this promise, "If any of you lack wisdom, let him ask of God . . . and it shall be given him" (James 1:5). God cares about every issue that we face daily, and He will give direction *if* we take time to ask Him.

God's plan for us may not meet our limited expectations, but it will certainly, in some way, exceed them. Like a sunflower, you can grow and bloom in the care of your heavenly Father. *And that is ideal.*

A B O U T **S U E**

The Daily Planner was designed by Sue Hooley, wife of Dan for 27 years and mother to six children, two girls and four boys ages 8-24. The planner was developed after several years of motherhood and homemaking. Sue understood that a homemaker's day can rarely be scheduled and structured the same as the one before, nor can every task fit neatly into the time slot allotted by other planners. Since her first publication in 2010, thousands of homemakers have benefited from the Daily Planner.

If you have comments about the Daily Planner, you may share your thoughts by sending an e-mail to: *office@homemakersdepot.com*
or writing to: **Sue Hooley 3176A Bulldog Creek Road, Valley, WA 99181.**
To read more, visit **www.homemakersdepot.com**

If you like this planner, help us out by leaving a review on Amazon.

NEED A HAND WITH
MENU PLANNING?

Download a free copy of 2018 Homemaker's Friend Menu Planning Worksheets Today!

Have you stood in front of the refrigerator door and wondered desperately what to make for dinner? *Homemaker's Friend Menu Planning Worksheets* will help you plan your menus much more easily. Instead of spending much-needed brain power each day trying to think what to make for the next meal, free up your mind and your time to focus on other things.

Menu planning requires forethought but saves time in the long run. It is a work in progress that takes practice, but the more you do it, the easier it will become.

Try these Menu Planning Worksheets at no risk, and . . .

- Make grocery shopping easier.
- Create balanced meals with more variety.
- Save money by planning in advance.
- Add flexibility to your meal schedule.
- Become more likely to try new recipes.
- Take advantage of sale items.

Size: 8.5" x 11"

TO REQUEST YOUR
FREE PRINTABLE PDF,
send an e-mail to:
office@homemakersdepot.com
or download it from our website at *www.homemakersdepot.com.*

THE FLEXIBLE PLANNER **FOR HOMEMAKERS**

Twenty years ago when I was a young homemaker, I read *Getting More Done in Less Time* by Donna Otto. She recommended using a simple daily planner to keep track of duties, appointments, and commitments. "It will be your friend for life," she promised.

I began my search for a planner that would help me organize my days and duties. But I soon realized that my homemaking days did not fit into neat little time slots. It was frustrating to be rocking the baby at 10:00 when the planner said, "Weed flower bed." So I started designing my own planner pages so that I could have flexible plan.

Today *The Homemaker's Friend Daily Planner* is a professional version of those homemade pages of years gone by. Through eleven moves, from one child to six, from toddlers to adult children, this basic, flexible planner kept me on track while allowing me to change from one stage to the next.

> Write with a pencil so tasks can easily be erased and rearranged.

The planner is divided into the following sections.

WEEKLY PLANNING. This user-friendly section helps you make the most out of your week and day. The "Task List" gives you a visual of what needs to be done, and you can divvy out those duties on specific days. Typically, I use a four-week menu plan, but I still write what is for dinner in the menu block.

MONTHLY CALENDAR. This section gives an overall view of events on the horizon. This helps me to be more realistic with weekly planning, since I can see at a glance what will be happening over the next few weeks.

> Complete the most important tasks first for the day or week to boost productivity.

YEARLY CALENDAR. This section has a place for basic notations. Now with the 52 untitled sections, you have a place to journal or write prayer requests, birthdays, and quotes.

TASKS LIST. These pages are untitled to give you the freedom to create monthly, bimonthly, or seasonal lists.

PROJECTS AND EVENTS. This section is for occasions that need more space for writing like when planning a baby shower or a family gathering. Again, these pages are untitled for flexibility.

A visual outline of your completed and uncompleted tasks helps you be more organized and stay focused.

INFORMATION. This section can be used for phone numbers and addresses that are needed temporarily, such as an address for a card shower or the information for the eye specialist.

SHOPPING LISTS. These lists are perforated for your convenience. I use the shopping lists several ways—sometimes as a comprehensive shopping list and other times as a central location for items needed for an upcoming event, project, or menu.

A running shopping list helps you to make the best of a trip to town.

The busier I am, the more I use my planner. It helps me balance homemaking responsibilities with other obligations to create a realistic schedule. Though it is typical for me to veer from a daily plan when urgent matters arise, a written plan refreshes my memory. Mrs. Otto was right—my planner is a lifetime friend.

YEARLY
GOALS

_____

_____

_____

_____

_____

_____

_____

_____

_____

_____

_____

_____

_____

_____

_____

_____

_____

_____

_____

_____

_____

_____

_____

_____

2018 MINI CALENDARS

JANUARY

S	M	T	W	T	F	S
	1	2	3	4	5	6
7	8	9	10	11	12	13
14	15	16	17	18	19	20
21	22	23	24	25	26	27
28	29	30	31			

FEBRUARY

S	M	T	W	T	F	S
				1	2	3
4	5	6	7	8	9	10
11	12	13	14	15	16	17
18	19	20	21	22	23	24
25	26	27	28			

MARCH

S	M	T	W	T	F	S
				1	2	3
4	5	6	7	8	9	10
11	12	13	14	15	16	17
18	19	20	21	22	23	24
25	26	27	28	29	30	31

APRIL

S	M	T	W	T	F	S
1	2	3	4	5	6	7
8	9	10	11	12	13	14
15	16	17	18	19	20	21
22	23	24	25	26	27	28
29	30					

MAY

S	M	T	W	T	F	S
		1	2	3	4	5
6	7	8	9	10	11	12
13	14	15	16	17	18	19
20	21	22	23	24	25	26
27	28	29	30	31		

JUNE

S	M	T	W	T	F	S
					1	2
3	4	5	6	7	8	9
10	11	12	13	14	15	16
17	18	19	20	21	22	23
24	25	26	27	28	29	30

JULY

S	M	T	W	T	F	S
1	2	3	4	5	6	7
8	9	10	11	12	13	14
15	16	17	18	19	20	21
22	23	24	25	26	27	28
29	30	31				

AUGUST

S	M	T	W	T	F	S
			1	2	3	4
5	6	7	8	9	10	11
12	13	14	15	16	17	18
19	20	21	22	23	24	25
26	27	28	29	30	31	

SEPTEMBER

S	M	T	W	T	F	S
						1
2	3	4	5	6	7	8
9	10	11	12	13	14	15
16	17	18	19	20	21	22
23 30	24	25	26	27	28	29

OCTOBER

S	M	T	W	T	F	S
	1	2	3	4	5	6
7	8	9	10	11	12	13
14	15	16	17	18	19	20
21	22	23	24	25	26	27
28	29	30	31			

NOVEMBER

S	M	T	W	T	F	S
				1	2	3
4	5	6	7	8	9	10
11	12	13	14	15	16	17
18	19	20	21	22	23	24
25	26	27	28	29	30	

DECEMBER

S	M	T	W	T	F	S
						1
2	3	4	5	6	7	8
9	10	11	12	13	14	15
16	17	18	19	20	21	22
23 30	24 31	25	26	27	28	29

2018 DATES TO REMEMBER

JANUARY

FEBRUARY

MARCH

APRIL

MAY

JUNE

JULY

AUGUST

SEPTEMBER

OCTOBER

NOVEMBER

DECEMBER

2019 MINI CALENDARS

JANUARY

S	M	T	W	T	F	S
		1	2	3	4	5
6	7	8	9	10	11	12
13	14	15	16	17	18	19
20	21	22	23	24	25	26
27	28	29	30	31		

FEBRUARY

S	M	T	W	T	F	S
					1	2
3	4	5	6	7	8	9
10	11	12	13	14	15	16
17	18	19	20	21	22	23
24	25	26	27	28		

MARCH

S	M	T	W	T	F	S
					1	2
3	4	5	6	7	8	9
10	11	12	13	14	15	16
17	18	19	20	21	22	23
24 31	25	26	27	28	29	30

APRIL

S	M	T	W	T	F	S
	1	2	3	4	5	6
7	8	9	10	11	12	13
14	15	16	17	18	19	20
21	22	23	24	25	26	27
28	29	30				

MAY

S	M	T	W	T	F	S
			1	2	3	4
5	6	7	8	9	10	11
12	13	14	15	16	17	18
19	20	21	22	23	24	25
26	27	28	29	30	31	

JUNE

S	M	T	W	T	F	S
						1
2	3	4	5	6	7	8
9	10	11	12	13	14	15
16	17	18	19	20	21	22
23 30	24	25	26	27	28	29

JULY

S	M	T	W	T	F	S
	1	2	3	4	5	6
7	8	9	10	11	12	13
14	15	16	17	18	19	20
21	22	23	24	25	26	27
28	29	30	31			

AUGUST

S	M	T	W	T	F	S
				1	2	3
4	5	6	7	8	9	10
11	12	13	14	15	16	17
18	19	20	21	22	23	24
25	26	27	28	29	30	31

SEPTEMBER

S	M	T	W	T	F	S
1	2	3	4	5	6	7
8	9	10	11	12	13	14
15	16	17	18	19	20	21
22	23	24	25	26	27	28
29	30					

OCTOBER

S	M	T	W	T	F	S
		1	2	3	4	5
6	7	8	9	10	11	12
13	14	15	16	17	18	19
20	21	22	23	24	25	26
27	28	29	30	31		

NOVEMBER

S	M	T	W	T	F	S
					1	2
3	4	5	6	7	8	9
10	11	12	13	14	15	16
17	18	19	20	21	22	23
24	25	26	27	28	29	30

DECEMBER

S	M	T	W	T	F	S
1	2	3	4	5	6	7
8	9	10	11	12	13	14
15	16	17	18	19	20	21
22	23	24	25	26	27	28
29	30	31				

2019 DATES TO REMEMBER

JANUARY
_____
_____
_____
_____
_____

FEBRUARY
_____
_____
_____
_____
_____

MARCH
_____
_____
_____
_____
_____

APRIL
_____
_____
_____
_____
_____

MAY
_____
_____
_____
_____
_____

JUNE
_____
_____
_____
_____
_____

JULY
_____
_____
_____
_____
_____

AUGUST
_____
_____
_____
_____
_____

SEPTEMBER
_____
_____
_____
_____
_____

OCTOBER
_____
_____
_____
_____
_____

NOVEMBER
_____
_____
_____
_____
_____

DECEMBER
_____
_____
_____
_____
_____

PERSONALIZE THESE PAGES

for journaling, prayer requests, birthdays, etc.

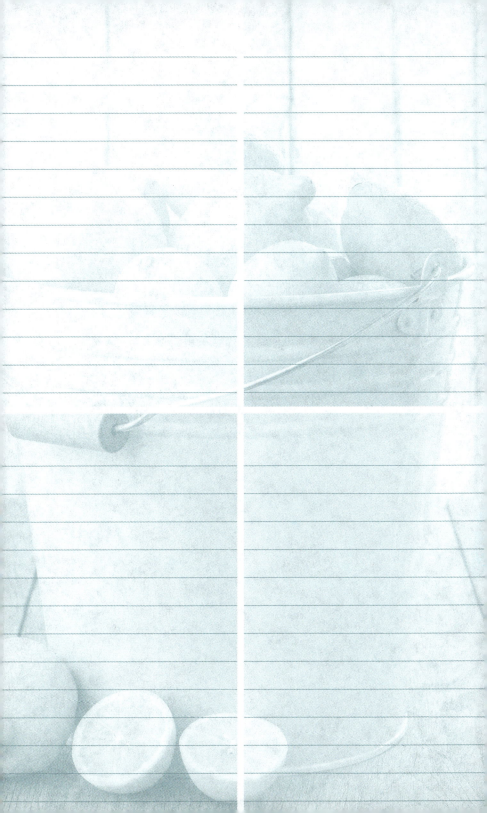

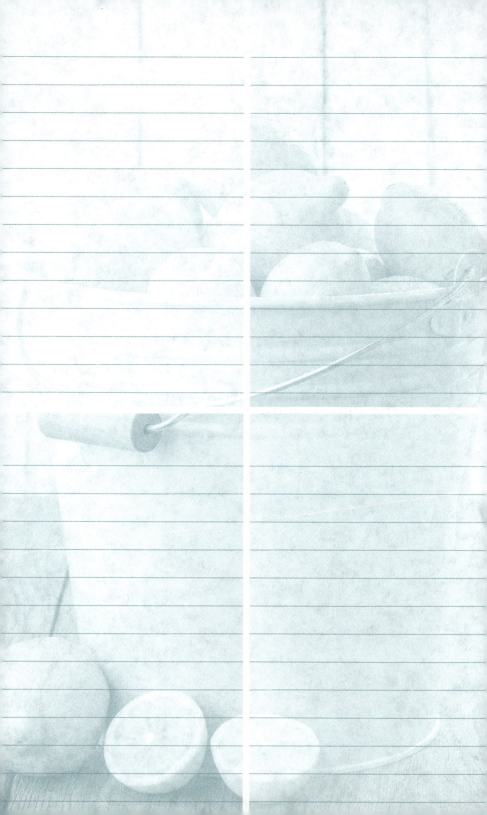

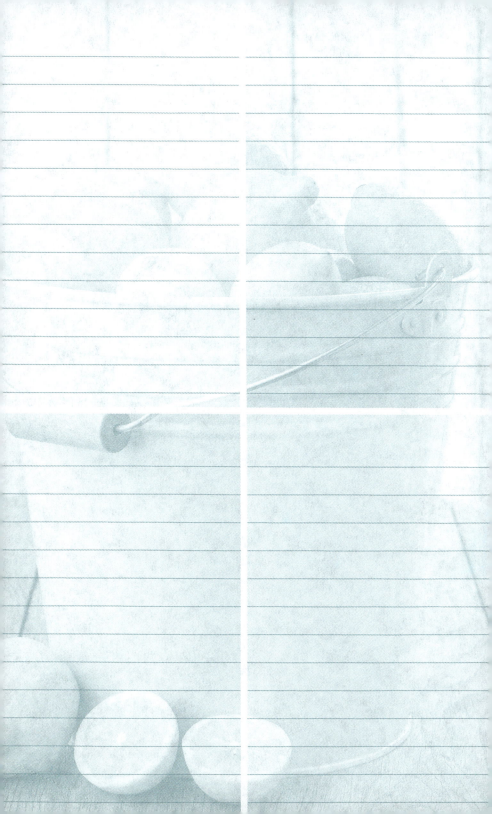

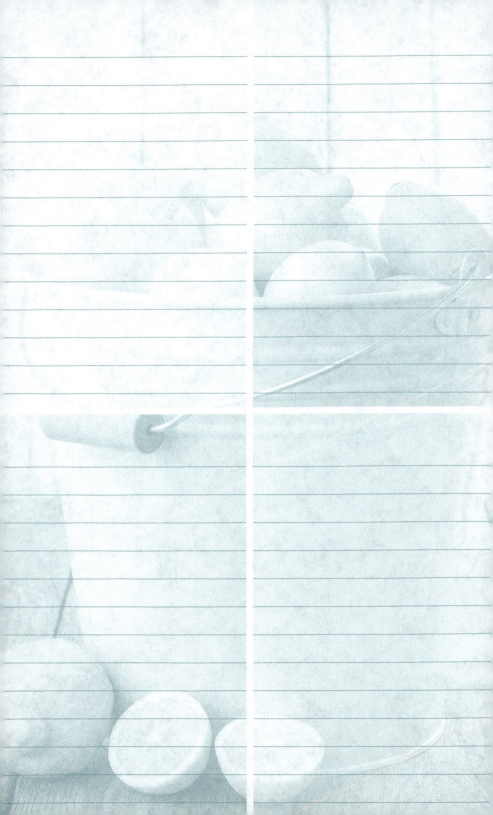

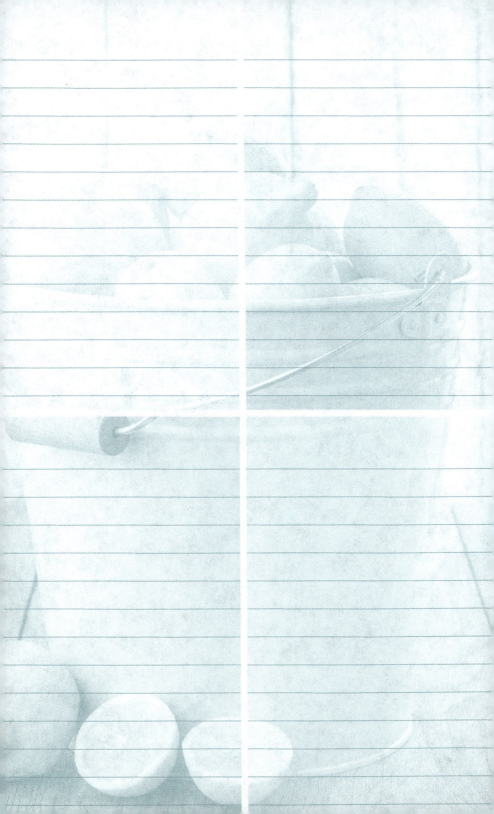

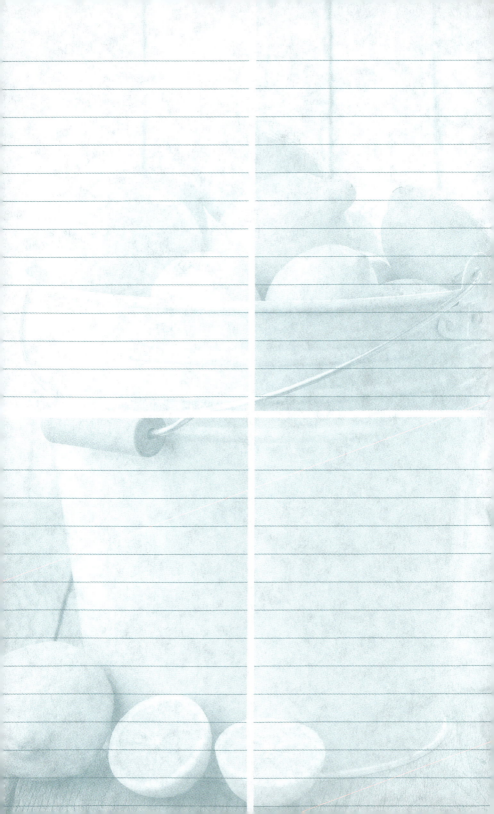

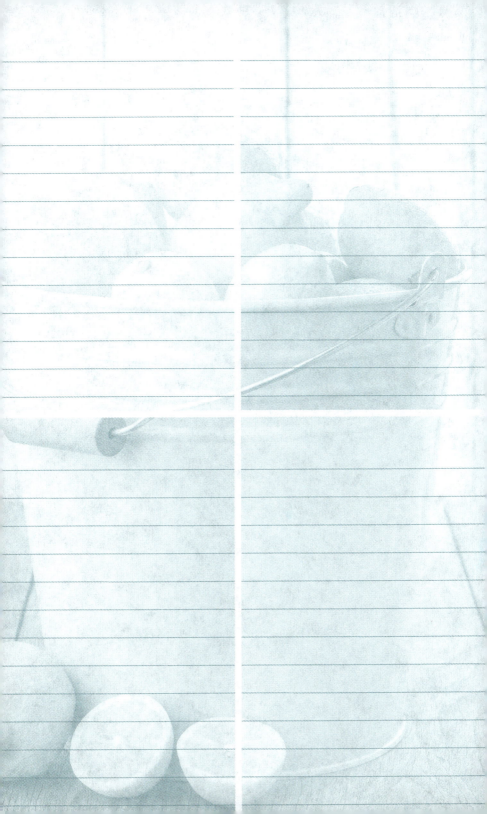

MONTHLY
GOALS

_____
_____
_____
_____
_____
_____
_____
_____
_____
_____
_____
_____
_____
_____
_____
_____
_____
_____
_____
_____
_____
_____
_____
_____
_____
_____

JANUARY

two thousand eighteen

SUNDAY	MONDAY	TUESDAY
	1	2
	New Year's Day	
7	8	9
14	15	16
	Martin Luther King Jr. Day	
21	22	23
28	29	30

NOTES

_____

_____

_____

_____

_____

_____

_____

_____

_____

_____

_____

_____

_____

DECEMBER 17

S	M	T	W	T	F	S
					1	2
3	4	5	6	7	8	9
10	11	12	13	14	15	16
17	18	19	20	21	22	23
24	25	26	27	28	29	30
31						

FEBRUARY

S	M	T	W	T	F	S
				1	2	3
4	5	6	7	8	9	10
11	12	13	14	15	16	17
18	19	20	21	22	23	24
25	26	27	28			

WEDNESDAY	THURSDAY	FRIDAY	SATURDAY
3	4	5	6
10	11	12	13
17	18	19	20
24	25	26	27
31			

FEBRUARY
two thousand eighteen

SUNDAY	MONDAY	TUESDAY
4	5	6
11	12	13
18	19 Presidents' Day	20
25	26	27

NOTES

_____
_____
_____
_____
_____
_____
_____
_____
_____
_____
_____
_____
_____
_____
_____
_____
_____

JANUARY						
S	M	T	W	T	F	S
	1	2	3	4	5	6
7	8	9	10	11	12	13
14	15	16	17	18	19	20
21	22	23	24	25	26	27
28	29	30	31			

MARCH						
S	M	T	W	T	F	S
				1	2	3
4	5	6	7	8	9	10
11	12	13	14	15	16	17
18	19	20	21	22	23	24
25	26	27	28	29	30	31

WEDNESDAY	THURSDAY	FRIDAY	SATURDAY
	1	2 Groundhog Day	3
7	8	9	10
14 Valentine's Day Ash Wednesday	15	16	17
21	22	23	24
28			

Cut along line to expose tabs.

M A R C H
two thousand eighteen

SUNDAY	MONDAY	TUESDAY
4	5	6
11	12	13
Daylight Saving Time Begins		
18	19	20
25	26	27
Palm Sunday		

N O T E S

FEBRUARY	S	M	T	W	T	F	S
					1	2	3
	4	5	6	7	8	9	10
	11	12	13	14	15	16	17
	18	19	20	21	22	23	24
	25	26	27	28			

APRIL	S	M	T	W	T	F	S
	1	2	3	4	5	6	7
	8	9	10	11	12	13	14
	15	16	17	18	19	20	21
	22	23	24	25	26	27	28
	29	30					

WEDNESDAY	THURSDAY	FRIDAY	SATURDAY
	1	2	3
7	8	9	10
14	15	16	17 St. Patrick's Day
21	22	23	24
28	29	30 Good Friday	31

Cut along dotted line to expose tabs.

APRIL
two thousand eighteen

NOTES

SUNDAY	MONDAY	TUESDAY
1 Easter	2	3
8	9	10
15	16	17
22	23	24
29	30	

MARCH

S	M	T	W	T	F	S
				1	2	3
4	5	6	7	8	9	10
11	12	13	14	15	16	17
18	19	20	21	22	23	24
25	26	27	28	29	30	31

MAY

S	M	T	W	T	F	S
		1	2	3	4	5
6	7	8	9	10	11	12
13	14	15	16	17	18	19
20	21	22	23	24	25	26
27	28	29	30	31		

WEDNESDAY	THURSDAY	FRIDAY	SATURDAY
4	5	6	7
11	12	13	14
18	19	20	21
25	26	27	28

APRIL

Cut along dotted line to expose tabs.

MAY
two thousand eighteen

NOTES

SUNDAY	MONDAY	TUESDAY
		1
6	7	8
13 Mother's Day	14	15
20	21	22
27	28 Memorial Day	29

APRIL	S	M	T	W	T	F	S
	1	2	3	4	5	6	7
	8	9	10	11	12	13	14
	15	16	17	18	19	20	21
	22	23	24	25	26	27	28
	29	30					

JUNE	S	M	T	W	T	F	S
						1	2
	3	4	5	6	7	8	9
	10	11	12	13	14	15	16
	17	18	19	20	21	22	23
	24	25	26	27	28	29	30

WEDNESDAY	THURSDAY	FRIDAY	SATURDAY
2	3	4	5
9	10	11	12
16	17	18	19
23	24	25	26
30	31		

MAY

Cut along dotted line to expose tabs.

JUNE

two thousand eighteen

NOTES

SUNDAY	MONDAY	TUESDAY
3	4	5
10	11	12
17	18	19
Father's Day		
24	25	26

	S	M	T	W	T	F	S
MAY			1	2	3	4	5
	6	7	8	9	10	11	12
	13	14	15	16	17	18	19
	20	21	22	23	24	25	26
	27	28	29	30	31		

	S	M	T	W	T	F	S
JULY	1	2	3	4	5	6	7
	8	9	10	11	12	13	14
	15	16	17	18	19	20	21
	22	23	24	25	26	27	28
	29	30	31				

WEDNESDAY	THURSDAY	FRIDAY	SATURDAY
		1	2
6	7	8	9
13	14	15	16
20	21	22	23
27	28	29	30

JUNE

Cut along dotted line to expose tabs.

JULY
two thousand eighteen

SUNDAY	MONDAY	TUESDAY
1	2	3
8	9	10
15	16	17
22	23	24
29	30	31

NOTES

_____
_____
_____
_____
_____
_____
_____
_____
_____
_____
_____
_____
_____
_____
_____

	S	M	T	W	T	F	S
JUNE						1	2
	3	4	5	6	7	8	9
	10	11	12	13	14	15	16
	17	18	19	20	21	22	23
	24	25	26	27	28	29	30

	S	M	T	W	T	F	S
AUGUST				1	2	3	4
	5	6	7	8	9	10	11
	12	13	14	15	16	17	18
	19	20	21	22	23	24	25
	26	27	28	29	30	31	

WEDNESDAY	THURSDAY	FRIDAY	SATURDAY
4 Independence Day	5	6	7
11	12	13	14
18	19	20	21
25	26	27	28

JULY

Cut along dotted line to expose tabs.

AUGUST
two thousand eighteen

SUNDAY	MONDAY	TUESDAY
5	6	7
12	13	14
19	20	21
26	27	28

NOTES

_____

_____

_____

_____

_____

_____

_____

_____

_____

_____

_____

_____

_____

JULY

S	M	T	W	T	F	S
1	2	3	4	5	6	7
8	9	10	11	12	13	14
15	16	17	18	19	20	21
22	23	24	25	26	27	28
29	30	31				

SEPTEMBER

S	M	T	W	T	F	S
						1
2	3	4	5	6	7	8
9	10	11	12	13	14	15
16	17	18	19	20	21	22
23 30	24	25	26	27	28	29

WEDNESDAY	THURSDAY	FRIDAY	SATURDAY
1	2	3	4
8	9	10	11
15	16	17	18
22	23	24	25
29	30	31	

AUGUST

Cut along dotted line to expose tabs.

SEPTEMBER

two thousand eighteen

SUNDAY	MONDAY	TUESDAY
2	3	4
	Labor Day	
9	10	11
16	17	18
23	24	25
30		

NOTES

_____

_____

_____

_____

_____

_____

_____

_____

_____

_____

_____

_____

_____

AUGUST

S	M	T	W	T	F	S
			1	2	3	4
5	6	7	8	9	10	11
12	13	14	15	16	17	18
19	20	21	22	23	24	25
26	27	28	29	30	31	

OCTOBER

S	M	T	W	T	F	S
	1	2	3	4	5	6
7	8	9	10	11	12	13
14	15	16	17	18	19	20
21	22	23	24	25	26	27
28	29	30	31			

WEDNESDAY	THURSDAY	FRIDAY	SATURDAY
			1
5	6	7	8
12	13	14	15
19	20	21	22
26	27	28	29

SEPTEMBER

OCTOBER
two thousand eighteen

NOTES

_____

_____

_____

_____

_____

_____

_____

_____

_____

_____

_____

_____

_____

_____

SUNDAY	MONDAY	TUESDAY
	1	2
7	8 Columbus Day	9
14	15	16
21	22	23
28	29	30

SEPTEMBER

S	M	T	W	T	F	S
						1
2	3	4	5	6	7	8
9	10	11	12	13	14	15
16	17	18	19	20	21	22
23 30	24	25	26	27	28	29

NOVEMBER

S	M	T	W	T	F	S
				1	2	3
4	5	6	7	8	9	10
11	12	13	14	15	16	17
18	19	20	21	22	23	24
25	26	27	28	29	30	

WEDNESDAY	THURSDAY	FRIDAY	SATURDAY
3	4	5	6
10	11	12	13
17	18	19	20
24	25	26	27
31			

OCTOBER

NOVEMBER
two thousand eighteen

SUNDAY	MONDAY	TUESDAY
4 Daylight Saving Time Ends	5	6
11 Veteran's Day	12 Veteran's Day Observed	13
18	19	20
25	26	27

NOTES

_____

_____

_____

_____

_____

_____

_____

_____

_____

_____

_____

_____

_____

OCTOBER

S	M	T	W	T	F	S
	1	2	3	4	5	6
7	8	9	10	11	12	13
14	15	16	17	18	19	20
21	22	23	24	25	26	27
28	29	30	31			

DECEMBER

S	M	T	W	T	F	S
						1
2	3	4	5	6	7	8
9	10	11	12	13	14	15
16	17	18	19	20	21	22
23 30	24 31	25	26	27	28	29

WEDNESDAY	THURSDAY	FRIDAY	SATURDAY
	1	2	3
7	8	9	10
14	15	16	17
21	22 Thanksgiving Day	23	24
28	29	30	

DECEMBER
two thousand eighteen

SUNDAY	MONDAY	TUESDAY
2	3	4
9	10	11
16	17	18
23	24 Christmas Eve	25
30	31 New Year's Eve	Christmas Day

NOTES

_____

_____

_____

_____

_____

_____

_____

_____

_____

_____

_____

_____

_____

_____

NOVEMBER

S	M	T	W	T	F	S
				1	2	3
4	5	6	7	8	9	10
11	12	13	14	15	16	17
18	19	20	21	22	23	24
25	26	27	28	29	30	

JANUARY 19

S	M	T	W	T	F	S
		1	2	3	4	5
6	7	8	9	10	11	12
13	14	15	16	17	18	19
20	21	22	23	24	25	26
27	28	29	30	31		

WEDNESDAY	THURSDAY	FRIDAY	SATURDAY
			1
5	6	7	8
12	13	14	15
19	20	21	22
26	27	28	29

NOTES

WEEKLY
GOALS

TASKS LIST

I will be glad and rejoice in thy mercy:
for thou hast considered my trouble;
thou hast known my soul in adversities.
PSALM 31:7

DECEMBER						1	2
3	4	5	6	7	8	9
10	11	12	13	14	15	16
17	18	19	20	21	22	23
24	25	26	27	28	29	30
31						

MONDAY 4

MENU:

TUESDAY 5

MENU:

WEDNESDAY 6

MENU:

THURSDAY 7

MENU:

FRIDAY 8

MENU:

SATURDAY 9

SUNDAY 10

MENU:

MENU:

TASKS LIST

Be thou exalted, LORD, in thine
own strength: so will we sing and
praise thy power.
PSALM 21:13

DECEMBER

					1	2
3	4	5	6	7	8	9
10	11	12	13	14	15	16
17	18	19	20	21	22	23
24	25	26	27	28	29	30
31						

MONDAY 11

MENU:

TUESDAY 12

MENU:

WEDNESDAY 13

MENU:

THURSDAY 14

MENU:

FRIDAY 15

MENU:

SATURDAY 16

MENU:

SUNDAY 17

MENU:

TASKS LIST

Rejoice in the LORD, O ye righteous:
for praise is comely for the upright.
PSALM 33:1

DECEMBER

					1	2
3	4	5	6	7	8	9
10	11	12	13	14	15	16
17	18	19	20	21	22	23
24	25	26	27	28	29	30
31						

MONDAY 18

MENU:

TUESDAY 19

MENU:

cut here

WEDNESDAY 20

MENU:

THURSDAY 21

MENU:

FRIDAY 22

MENU:

SATURDAY 23

MENU:

SUNDAY 24

CHRISTMAS EVE

MENU:

TASKS LIST

And the angel said unto them, Fear not: for, behold, I bring you good tidings of great joy, which shall be to all people. For unto you is born this day in the city of David a Saviour, which is Christ the Lord.
LUKE 2:10, 11

DECEMBER

					1	2
3	4	5	6	7	8	9
10	11	12	13	14	15	16
17	18	19	20	21	22	23
24	25	26	27	28	29	30
31						

MONDAY 25

CHRISTMAS DAY

MENU:

TUESDAY 26

MENU:

cut here

WEDNESDAY 27

MENU:

THURSDAY 28

MENU:

FRIDAY 29

MENU:

SATURDAY 30

MENU:

SUNDAY 31

NEW YEAR'S EVE

MENU:

January 1 » January 7

From the rising of the sun unto
the going down of the same the
LORD'S name is to be praised.
P S A L M   1 1 3 : 3

JANUARY

	1	2	3	4	5	6
7	8	9	10	11	12	13
14	15	16	17	18	19	20
21	22	23	24	25	26	27
28	29	30	31			

MONDAY 1

NEW YEAR'S DAY

M E N U :

TUESDAY 2

M E N U :

WEDNESDAY 3

MENU:

THURSDAY 4

MENU:

FRIDAY 5

MENU:

SATURDAY 6

SUNDAY 7

MENU:

MENU:

TASKS LIST

January 8 » January 14

_____   _____
_____   _____
_____   _____
_____   _____
_____   _____
_____   _____
_____   _____
_____   _____
_____   _____

I will sing unto the LORD,
because he hath dealt bountifully
with me.
PSALM 13:6

JANUARY						
	1	2	3	4	5	6
7	8	9	10	11	12	13
14	15	16	17	18	19	20
21	22	23	24	25	26	27
28	29	30	31			

MONDAY 8

MENU:

TUESDAY 9

MENU:

WEDNESDAY 10

MENU:

THURSDAY 11

MENU:

FRIDAY 12

MENU:

SATURDAY 13

SUNDAY 14

MENU:

MENU:

TASKS LIST

January 15 » January 21

> I will praise thee, O LORD, with my whole heart; I will shew forth all thy marvellous works.
>
> PSALM 9:1

JANUARY						
	1	2	3	4	5	6
7	8	9	10	11	12	13
14	15	16	17	18	19	20
21	22	23	24	25	26	27
28	29	30	31			

MONDAY 15

MARTIN LUTHER KING JR. DAY

MENU:

TUESDAY 16

MENU:

WEDNESDAY 17

MENU:

THURSDAY 18

MENU:

FRIDAY 19

MENU:

SATURDAY 20

SUNDAY 21

MENU:

MENU:

TASKS LIST

January 22 » January 28

_____   _____
_____   _____
_____   _____
_____   _____
_____   _____
_____   _____
_____   _____

**Let all those that seek thee rejoice and be
glad in thee: let such as love thy salvation
say continually, The LORD be magnified.**
PSALM 40:16

JANUARY					
	1	2	3	4	5	6
7	8	9	10	11	12	13
14	15	16	17	18	19	20
21	22	23	24	25	26	27
28	29	30	31			

MONDAY 22

MENU:

TUESDAY 23

MENU:

WEDNESDAY 24

MENU:

THURSDAY 25

MENU:

FRIDAY 26

MENU:

SATURDAY 27

SUNDAY 28

MENU:

MENU:

TASKS LIST

January 29 » February 4

I will praise the LORD according to his
righteousness: and will sing praise to the
name of the LORD most high.
PSALM 7:17

JANUARY						
	1	2	3	4	5	6
7	8	9	10	11	12	13
14	15	16	17	18	19	20
21	22	23	24	25	26	27
28	29	30	31	*1*	*2*	*3*
4						

MONDAY 29

MENU:

TUESDAY 30

MENU:

WEDNESDAY 31

MENU:

THURSDAY 1

MENU:

FRIDAY 2

GROUNDHOG DAY

MENU:

SATURDAY 3

SUNDAY 4

MENU:

MENU:

TASKS LIST

February 5 » February 11

_____

_____

_____

_____

_____

_____

_____

_____

My meditation of him shall be sweet:
I will be glad in the LORD.
PSALM 104:34

FEBRUARY

					1	2	3
4	5	6	7	8	9	10
11	12	13	14	15	16	17
18	19	20	21	22	23	24
25	26	27	28			

MONDAY 5

MENU:

TUESDAY 6

MENU:

WEDNESDAY 7

MENU:

THURSDAY 8

MENU:

FRIDAY 9

MENU:

SATURDAY 10

SUNDAY 11

MENU:

MENU:

TASKS LIST

February 12 » February 18

Sing unto the LORD, O ye saints of his, and give thanks at the remembrance of his holiness.

PSALM 30:4

FEBRUARY

				1	2	3
4	5	6	7	8	9	10
11	12	13	14	15	16	17
18	19	20	21	22	23	24
25	26	27	28			

MONDAY 12

MENU:

TUESDAY 13

MENU:

WEDNESDAY 14

VALENTINE'S DAY

ASH WEDNESDAY

MENU:

THURSDAY 15

MENU:

FRIDAY 16

MENU:

SATURDAY 17

MENU:

SUNDAY 18

MENU:

February 19 » February 25

My tongue shall speak of thy
righteousness and of thy praise
all the day long.
P S A L M   3 5 : 2 8

M O N D A Y 19

PRESIDENTS' DAY

M E N U :

T U E S D A Y 20

M E N U :

cut here

WEDNESDAY 21

MENU:

THURSDAY 22

MENU:

FRIDAY 23

MENU:

SATURDAY 24

SUNDAY 25

MENU:

MENU:

TASKS LIST

February 26 » March 4

_____
_____
_____
_____
_____
_____
_____
_____
_____

_____
_____
_____
_____
_____
_____
_____
_____
_____

But thanks be to God, which giveth us the victory through our Lord Jesus Christ.
1 CORINTHIANS 15:57

FEBRUARY						
				1	2	3
4	5	6	7	8	9	10
11	12	13	14	15	16	17
18	19	20	21	22	23	24
25	26	27	28	1	2	3
4						

MONDAY 26

MENU:

TUESDAY 27

MENU:

WEDNESDAY 28

MENU:

THURSDAY 1

MENU:

FRIDAY 2

MENU:

SATURDAY 3

SUNDAY 4

MENU:

MENU:

TASKS LIST

March 5 » March 11

_____

_____

_____

_____

_____

_____

_____

_____

_____

Be glad in the LORD, and rejoice,
ye righteous: and shout for joy,
all ye that are upright in heart.
PSALM 32:11

MARCH					1	2	3
4	5	6	7	8	9	10
11	12	13	14	15	16	17
18	19	20	21	22	23	24
25	26	27	28	29	30	31

MONDAY 5

MENU:

TUESDAY 6

MENU:

cut here

WEDNESDAY 7

MENU:

THURSDAY 8

MENU:

FRIDAY 9

MENU:

SATURDAY 10

SUNDAY 11

DAYLIGHT SAVINGS TIME BEGINS

MENU:

MENU:

TASKS LIST

March 12 » March 18

I will bless the LORD at all times: his
praise shall continually be in my mouth...
O magnify the LORD with me,
and let us exalt his name together.
PSALM 34:1

MARCH						
			1	2	3	
4	5	6	7	8	9	10
11	12	13	14	15	16	17
18	19	20	21	22	23	24
25	26	27	28	29	30	31

MONDAY 12

MENU:

TUESDAY 13

MENU:

WEDNESDAY 14

MENU:

THURSDAY 15

MENU:

FRIDAY 16

MENU:

SATURDAY 17

SUNDAY 18

ST. PATRICK'S DAY

MENU:

MENU:

TASKS LIST

March 19 » March 25

**In God we boast all the day long,
and praise thy name for ever. Selah.**
PSALM 44:8

					1	2	3
MARCH	4	5	6	7	8	9	10
	11	12	13	14	15	16	17
	18	19	20	21	22	23	24
	25	26	27	28	29	30	31

MONDAY 19

MENU:

TUESDAY 20

MENU:

WEDNESDAY 21

MENU:

THURSDAY 22

MENU:

FRIDAY 23

MENU:

SATURDAY 24

SUNDAY 25

PALM SUNDAY

MENU:

MENU:

TASKS LIST

March 26 » April 1

Worthy is the Lamb that was slain to
receive power, and riches, and wisdom,
and strength, and honour, and glory,
and blessing.
REVELATION 5:12

MARCH						
				1	2	3
4	5	6	7	8	9	10
11	12	13	14	15	16	17
18	19	20	21	22	23	24
25	26	27	28	29	30	31
1						

MONDAY 26

MENU:

TUESDAY 27

MENU:

cut here

WEDNESDAY 28

MENU:

THURSDAY 29

MENU:

FRIDAY 30

MENU:

GOOD FRIDAY

SATURDAY 31

SUNDAY 1

EASTER

MENU:

MENU:

TASKS LIST

April 2 » April 8

By him therefore let us offer the sacrifice
of praise to God continually, that is, the
fruit of our lips giving thanks to his name.
HEBREWS 13:15

APRIL

1	2	3	4	5	6	7
8	9	10	11	12	13	14
15	16	17	18	19	20	21
22	23	24	25	26	27	28
29	30					

MONDAY 2

MENU:

TUESDAY 3

MENU:

cut here

WEDNESDAY 4

MENU:

THURSDAY 5

MENU:

FRIDAY 6

MENU:

SATURDAY 7

MENU:

SUNDAY 8

MENU:

April 9 » April 15

Give unto the LORD the glory due
unto his name; worship the LORD in
the beauty of holiness.

PSALM 29:2

APRIL

1	2	3	4	5	6	7
8	9	10	11	12	13	14
15	16	17	18	19	20	21
22	23	24	25	26	27	28
29	30					

MONDAY 9

MENU:

TUESDAY 10

MENU:

WEDNESDAY 11

MENU:

THURSDAY 12

MENU:

FRIDAY 13

MENU:

SATURDAY 14

SUNDAY 15

MENU:

MENU:

TASKS LIST

April 16 » April 22

Sing unto the LORD;
for he hath done excellent things:
this is known in all the earth.
ISAIAH 12:5

APRIL						
1	2	3	4	5	6	7
8	9	10	11	12	13	14
15	16	17	18	19	20	21
22	23	24	25	26	27	28
29	30					

MONDAY 16

MENU:

TUESDAY 17

MENU:

WEDNESDAY **18**

MENU:

THURSDAY **19**

MENU:

FRIDAY **20**

MENU:

SATURDAY **21**

SUNDAY **22**

MENU:

MENU:

cut here

TASKS LIST

April 23 » April 29

But ye are a chosen generation, a royal priesthood, an holy nation, a peculiar people; that ye should shew forth the praises of him who hath called you out of darkness into his marvellous light.

1 PETER 2:9

APRIL						
1	2	3	4	5	6	7
8	9	10	11	12	13	14
15	16	17	18	19	20	21
22	23	24	25	26	27	28
29	30					

MONDAY 23

MENU:

TUESDAY 24

MENU:

WEDNESDAY 25

MENU:

THURSDAY 26

MENU:

FRIDAY 27

MENU:

SATURDAY 28

SUNDAY 29

MENU:

MENU:

TASKS LIST

April 30 » May 6

O give thanks unto the LORD;
for he is good:
for his mercy endureth for ever.
PSALM 136:1

MAY						
30	1	2	3	4	5
6	7	8	9	10	11	12
13	14	15	16	17	18	19
20	21	22	23	24	25	26
27	28	29	30	31		

MONDAY 30

MENU:

TUESDAY 1

MENU:

cut here

WEDNESDAY 2

MENU:

THURSDAY 3

MENU:

FRIDAY 4

MENU:

SATURDAY 5

SUNDAY 6

MENU:

MENU:

TASKS LIST

May 7 » May 13

Favour is deceitful, and beauty is
vain: but a woman that feareth the
LORD, she shall be praised.
P R O V E R B S   3 1 : 3 0

MAY						
		1	2	3	4	5
6	7	8	9	10	11	12
13	14	15	16	17	18	19
20	21	22	23	24	25	26
27	28	29	30	31		

MONDAY 7

MENU:

TUESDAY 8

MENU:

cut here

WEDNESDAY 9

MENU:

THURSDAY 10

MENU:

FRIDAY 11

MENU:

SATURDAY 12

SUNDAY 13

MOTHER'S DAY

MENU:

MENU:

TASKS LIST

May 14 » May 20

Rejoice in the LORD, ye righteous; and give thanks at the remembrance of his holiness.

PSALM 97:12

MAY						
		1	2	3	4	5
6	7	8	9	10	11	12
13	14	15	16	17	18	19
20	21	22	23	24	25	26
27	28	29	30	31		

MONDAY 14

MENU:

TUESDAY 15

MENU:

cut here

WEDNESDAY 16

MENU:

THURSDAY 17

MENU:

FRIDAY 18

MENU:

SATURDAY 19

SUNDAY 20

MENU:

MENU:

TASKS LIST

May 21 » May 27

Why art thou cast down, O my soul? and why art thou disquieted within me? hope in God: for I shall yet praise him, who is the health of my countenance, and my God.

PSALM 43:5

	1	2	3	4	5
6	7	8	9	10	11	12
13	14	15	16	17	18	19
20	21	22	23	24	25	26
27	28	29	30	31

MAY

MONDAY 21

MENU:

TUESDAY 22

MENU:

WEDNESDAY 23

MENU :

THURSDAY 24

MENU :

FRIDAY 25

MENU :

SATURDAY 26

SUNDAY 27

MENU :

MENU :

TASKS LIST

May 28 » June 3

I will praise the name of God with
a song, and will magnify him with
thanksgiving.
PSALM 69:30

		1	2	3	4	5
6	7	8	9	10	11	12
13	14	15	16	17	18	19
20	21	22	23	24	25	26
27	28	29	30	31	1	2
3						

MAY

MONDAY 28

MEMORIAL DAY

MENU:

TUESDAY 29

MENU:

WEDNESDAY 30

MENU:

THURSDAY 31

MENU:

FRIDAY 1

MENU:

SATURDAY 2

MENU:

SUNDAY 3

MENU:

TASKS LIST

June 4 » June 10

Thou art the God that doest wonders:
thou hast declared thy strength
among the people.
PSALM 77:14

						1	2
JUNE	3	4	5	6	7	8	9
	10	11	12	13	14	15	16
	17	18	19	20	21	22	23
	24	25	26	27	28	29	30

MONDAY 4

MENU:

TUESDAY 5

MENU:

WEDNESDAY 6

MENU:

THURSDAY 7

MENU:

FRIDAY 8

MENU:

SATURDAY 9

MENU:

SUNDAY 10

MENU:

TASKS LIST

June 11 » June 17

And he hath put a new song in my mouth,
even praise unto our God: many shall see it,
and fear, and shall trust in the LORD.
PSALM 40:3

JUNE

					1	2
3	4	5	6	7	8	9
10	11	12	13	14	15	16
17	18	19	20	21	22	23
24	25	26	27	28	29	30

MONDAY 11

MENU:

TUESDAY 12

MENU:

cut here

WEDNESDAY 13

MENU:

THURSDAY 14

MENU:

FRIDAY 15

MENU:

SATURDAY 16

MENU:

SUNDAY 17

FATHER'S DAY

MENU:

TASKS LIST

June 18 » June 24

In God I will praise his word,
in God I have put my trust; I will not
fear what flesh can do unto me.
PSALM 56:4

					1	2
3	4	5	6	7	8	9
10	11	12	13	14	15	16
17	18	19	20	21	22	23
24	25	26	27	28	29	30

JUNE

MONDAY 18

MENU:

TUESDAY 19

MENU:

WEDNESDAY 20

MENU:

THURSDAY 21

MENU:

FRIDAY 22

MENU:

SATURDAY 23

SUNDAY 24

MENU:

MENU:

TASKS LIST

June 25 » July 1

God is greatly to be feared in the assembly of
the saints, and to be had in reverence of all
them that are about him.
PSALM 89:7

JUNE					1	2
3	4	5	6	7	8	9
10	11	12	13	14	15	16
17	18	19	20	21	22	23
24	25	26	27	28	29	30
1						

MONDAY 25

MENU:

TUESDAY 26

MENU:

WEDNESDAY 27

MENU:

THURSDAY 28

MENU:

FRIDAY 29

MENU:

SATURDAY 30

SUNDAY 1

MENU:

MENU:

July 2 » July 8

Praise ye the LORD: for it is good to
sing praises unto our God;
for it is pleasant; and praise is comely.
PSALM 147:1

JULY

1	2	3	4	5	6	7
8	9	10	11	12	13	14
15	16	17	18	19	20	21
22	23	24	25	26	27	28
29	30	31				

MONDAY 2

MENU:

TUESDAY 3

MENU:

WEDNESDAY 4

INDEPENDENCE DAY

MENU:

THURSDAY 5

MENU:

FRIDAY 6

MENU:

SATURDAY 7

MENU:

SUNDAY 8

MENU:

TASKS LIST

July 9 » July 15

I will praise thee; for I am fearfully and
wonderfully made: marvellous are thy
works; and that my soul knoweth right well.
PSALM 139:14

JULY

1	2	3	4	5	6	7
8	9	10	11	12	13	14
15	16	17	18	19	20	21
22	23	24	25	26	27	28
29	30	31				

MONDAY 9

MENU:

TUESDAY 10

MENU:

WEDNESDAY 11

MENU:

THURSDAY 12

MENU:

FRIDAY 13

MENU:

SATURDAY 14

MENU:

SUNDAY 15

MENU:

TASKS LIST

July 16 » July 22

Saying, I will declare thy name unto my brethren, in the midst of the church will I sing praise unto thee.
HEBREWS 2:12

JULY

1	2	3	4	5	6	7
8	9	10	11	12	13	14
15	16	17	18	19	20	21
22	23	24	25	26	27	28
29	30	31				

MONDAY 16

MENU:

TUESDAY 17

MENU:

cut here

WEDNESDAY 18

MENU:

THURSDAY 19

MENU:

FRIDAY 20

MENU:

SATURDAY 21

SUNDAY 22

MENU:

MENU:

TASKS LIST

July 23 » July 29

_____
_____
_____
_____
_____
_____
_____
_____
_____

Give unto the LORD the glory due
unto his name; worship the LORD
in the beauty of holiness.
PSALM 29:2

JULY

1	2	3	4	5	6	7
8	9	10	11	12	13	14
15	16	17	18	19	20	21
22	23	24	25	26	27	28
29	30	31				

MONDAY 23

MENU:

TUESDAY 24

MENU:

cut here

WEDNESDAY 25

MENU :

THURSDAY 26

MENU :

FRIDAY 27

MENU :

SATURDAY 28

SUNDAY 29

MENU :

MENU :

TASKS LIST

July 30 » August 5

Who is like unto thee, O LORD, among the
gods? who is like thee, glorious in holiness,
fearful in praises, doing wonders?
EXODUS 15:11

AUGUST

	30	31	1	2	3	4
	5	6	7	8	9	10	11
	12	13	14	15	16	17	18
	19	20	21	22	23	24	25
	26	27	28	29	30	31	

MONDAY 30

MENU:

TUESDAY 31

MENU:

WEDNESDAY 1

MENU:

THURSDAY 2

MENU:

FRIDAY 3

MENU:

SATURDAY 4

MENU:

SUNDAY 5

MENU:

cut here

TASKS LIST

August 6 » August 12

For thou, LORD, hast made me glad through thy work: I will triumph in the works of thy hands.

PSALM 92:4

				1	2	3	4
AUGUST	5	6	7	8	9	10	11
	12	13	14	15	16	17	18
	19	20	21	22	23	24	25
	26	27	28	29	30	31	

MONDAY 6

MENU:

TUESDAY 7

MENU:

WEDNESDAY 8

MENU:

THURSDAY 9

MENU:

FRIDAY 10

MENU:

SATURDAY 11

ENU:

SUNDAY 12

MENU:

TASKS LIST

August 13 » August 19

Blessed be the God and Father of our
Lord Jesus Christ, who hath blessed us
with all spiritual blessings in heavenly
places in Christ.
EPHESIANS 1:3

				1	2	3	4
AUGUST	5	6	7	8	9	10	11
	12	13	14	15	16	17	18
	19	20	21	22	23	24	25
	26	27	28	29	30	31	

MONDAY 13

MENU:

TUESDAY 14

MENU:

WEDNESDAY 15

MENU:

THURSDAY 16

MENU:

FRIDAY 17

MENU:

SATURDAY 18

SUNDAY 19

MENU:

MENU:

TASKS LIST

August 20 » August 26

I will call on the LORD,
who is worthy to be praised:
so shall I be saved from mine enemies.
2 S A M U E L 2 2 : 4

AUGUST			1	2	3	4
5	6	7	8	9	10	11
12	13	14	15	16	17	18
19	20	21	22	23	24	25
26	27	28	29	30	31	

MONDAY 20

MENU:

TUESDAY 21

MENU:

cut here

WEDNESDAY 22

MENU:

THURSDAY 23

MENU:

FRIDAY 24

MENU:

SATURDAY 25

SUNDAY 26

MENU:

MENU:

TASKS LIST

August 27 » September 2

At midnight I will rise to give
thanks unto thee because of thy
righteous judgments.
PS 119:62

AUGUST						
			1	2	3	4
5	6	7	8	9	10	11
12	13	14	15	16	17	18
19	20	21	22	23	24	25
26	27	28	29	30	31	1
2						

MONDAY 27

MENU:

TUESDAY 28

MENU:

cut here

WEDNESDAY 29

MENU:

THURSDAY 30

MENU:

FRIDAY 31

MENU:

SATURDAY 1

SUNDAY 2

MENU:

MENU:

TASKS LIST

WEEK: *36*

September 3 » September 9

REMINDER:
Your 2019 Planner is available. *See order form in back*

O praise the LORD, all ye nations:
praise him, all ye people.
PS 117:1

SEPTEMBER

						1
2	3	4	5	6	7	8
9	10	11	12	13	14	15
16	17	18	19	20	21	22
23	24	25	26	27	28	29
30						

MONDAY 3

LABOR DAY

MENU:

TUESDAY 4

MENU:

cut here

WEDNESDAY 5

MENU:

THURSDAY 6

MENU:

FRIDAY 7

MENU:

SATURDAY 8

SUNDAY 9

MENU:

MENU:

September 10 » September 16

Seven times a day do I praise thee
because of thy righteous judgments.
PSALM 119:164

SEPTEMBER							1
	2	3	4	5	6	7	8
	9	10	11	12	13	14	15
	16	17	18	19	20	21	22
	23	24	25	26	27	28	29
	30						

MONDAY 10

MENU:

TUESDAY 11

MENU:

WEDNESDAY 12

MENU:

THURSDAY 13

MENU:

FRIDAY 14

MENU:

SATURDAY 15

MENU:

SUNDAY 16

MENU:

TASKS LIST

September 17 » September 23

_____   _____
_____   _____
_____   _____
_____   _____
_____   _____
_____   _____
_____   _____
_____   _____
_____   _____

For his merciful kindness is great
toward us: and the truth of the LORD
endureth for ever. Praise ye the LORD.
PSALM 117:2

SEPTEMBER						
						1
2	3	4	5	6	7	8
9	10	11	12	13	14	15
16	17	18	19	20	21	22
23	24	25	26	27	28	29
30						

MONDAY 17

_____
_____
_____
_____
_____

MENU:

TUESDAY 18

_____
_____
_____
_____
_____

MENU:

WEDNESDAY 19

MENU:

THURSDAY 20

MENU:

FRIDAY 21

MENU:

SATURDAY 22

MENU:

SUNDAY 23

MENU:

TASKS LIST

September 24 » September 30

_____ _____
_____ _____
_____ _____
_____ _____
_____ _____
_____ _____
_____ _____

Great is the LORD, and greatly to be praised; and his greatness is unsearchable.
PSALM 145:3

SEPTEMBER

						1
2	3	4	5	6	7	8
9	10	11	12	13	14	15
16	17	18	19	20	21	22
23	24	25	26	27	28	29
30						

MONDAY 24

_____
_____
_____
_____
_____
_____

MENU:

TUESDAY 25

_____
_____
_____
_____
_____

MENU:

WEDNESDAY 26

MENU:

THURSDAY 27

MENU:

FRIDAY 28

MENU:

SATURDAY 29

SUNDAY 30

MENU:

MENU:

TASKS LIST

October 1 » October 7

My soul shall make her boast in
the LORD: the humble shall hear
thereof, and be glad.
PSALM 34:2

OCTOBER	1	2	3	4	5	6
	7	8	9	10	11	12	13
	14	15	16	17	18	19	20
	21	22	23	24	25	26	27
	28	29	30	31			

MONDAY 1

MENU:

TUESDAY 2

MENU:

WEDNESDAY 3

MENU:

THURSDAY 4

MENU:

FRIDAY 5

MENU:

SATURDAY 6

SUNDAY 7

MENU:

MENU:

TASKS LIST

October 8 » October 14

But let the righteous be glad;
let them rejoice before God:
yea, let them exceedingly rejoice.
PSALM 68:3

OCTOBER

		1	2	3	4	5	6
7	8	9	10	11	12	13
14	15	16	17	18	19	20
21	22	23	24	25	26	27
28	29	30	31			

MONDAY 8

COLUMBUS DAY

MENU:

TUESDAY 9

MENU:

WEDNESDAY 10

MENU:

THURSDAY 11

MENU:

FRIDAY 12

MENU:

SATURDAY 13

SUNDAY 14

MENU:

MENU:

TASKS LIST

October 15 » October 21

Unto thee, O God, do we give thanks, unto
thee do we give thanks: for that thy name is
near thy wondrous works declare.
PSALM 75:1

OCTOBER						
	1	2	3	4	5	6
7	8	9	10	11	12	13
14	15	16	17	18	19	20
21	22	23	24	25	26	27
28	29	30	31			

MONDAY 15

MENU:

TUESDAY 16

MENU:

WEDNESDAY 17

MENU:

THURSDAY 18

MENU:

FRIDAY 19

MENU:

SATURDAY 20

SUNDAY 21

MENU:

MENU:

TASKS LIST

October 22 » October 28

The LORD hath done great things
for us; whereof we are glad.
PSALM 126:3

	1	2	3	4	5	6
7	8	9	10	11	12	13
14	15	16	17	18	19	20
21	22	23	24	25	26	27
28	29	30	31			

MONDAY 22

MENU:

TUESDAY 23

MENU:

WEDNESDAY 24

MENU:

THURSDAY 25

MENU:

FRIDAY 26

MENU:

SATURDAY 27

SUNDAY 28

MENU:

MENU:

TASKS LIST

October 29 » November 4

Rejoice, and be exceeding glad: for great is
your reward in heaven: for so persecuted
they the prophets which were before you.
MATTHEW 5:12

NOVEMBER

29	*30*	*31*	1	2	3
4	5	6	7	8	9	10
11	12	13	14	15	16	17
18	19	20	21	22	23	24
25	26	27	28	29	30	

MONDAY 29

MENU:

TUESDAY 30

MENU:

WEDNESDAY 31

MENU:

THURSDAY 1

MENU:

FRIDAY 2

MENU:

SATURDAY 3

MENU:

SUNDAY 4

DAYLIGHT SAVINGS TIME ENDS

MENU:

November 5 » November 11

Make me to hear joy and gladness;
that the bones which thou hast
broken may rejoice.
PSALM 51:8

NOVEMBER

					1	2	3
4	5	6	7	8	9	10
11	12	13	14	15	16	17
18	19	20	21	22	23	24
25	26	27	28	29	30

MONDAY 5

MENU:

TUESDAY 6

MENU:

WEDNESDAY 7

MENU:

THURSDAY 8

MENU:

FRIDAY 9

MENU:

SATURDAY 10

MENU:

SUNDAY 11

VETERAN'S DAY

MENU:

TASKS LIST

November 12 » November 18

_____ _____
_____ _____
_____ _____
_____ _____
_____ _____
_____ _____
_____ _____
_____ _____

**Enter into his gates with thanksgiving,
and into his courts with praise:
be thankful unto him, and bless his name.**
P S A L M   1 0 0 : 4

NOVEMBER

				1	2	3
4	5	6	7	8	9	10
11	12	13	14	15	16	17
18	19	20	21	22	23	24
25	26	27	28	29	30	

MONDAY 12

VETERAN'S DAY (OBSERVED)

M E N U :

TUESDAY 13

M E N U :

WEDNESDAY 14

MENU:

THURSDAY 15

MENU:

FRIDAY 16

MENU:

SATURDAY 17

SUNDAY 18

MENU:

MENU:

TASKS LIST

November 19 » November 25

In every thing give thanks: for this is the will of God in Christ Jesus concerning you.
1 THESSALONIANS 5:18

NOVEMBER

				1	2	3
4	5	6	7	8	9	10
11	12	13	14	15	16	17
18	19	20	21	22	23	24
25	26	27	28	29	30	

MONDAY 19

MENU:

TUESDAY 20

MENU:

WEDNESDAY 21

MENU:

THURSDAY 22

THANKSGIVING DAY

MENU:

FRIDAY 23

MENU:

SATURDAY 24

SUNDAY 25

MENU:

MENU:

TASKS LIST

November 26 » December 2

For thou, LORD, hast made me glad
through thy work: I will triumph
in the works of thy hands.
PSALM 92:4

NOVEMBER

				1	2	3
4	5	6	7	8	9	10
11	12	13	14	15	16	17
18	19	20	21	22	23	24
25	26	27	28	29	30	1
2						

MONDAY 26

MENU:

TUESDAY 27

MENU:

cut here

WEDNESDAY 28

MENU:

THURSDAY 29

MENU:

FRIDAY 30

MENU:

SATURDAY 1

SUNDAY 2

ENU:

MENU:

TASKS LIST

December 3 » December 9

Rejoice in the Lord alway:
and again I say, Rejoice.
PHILIPPIANS 4:4

DECEMBER

							1
	2	3	4	5	6	7	8
	9	10	11	12	13	14	15
	16	17	18	19	20	21	22
	23	24	25	26	27	28	29
	30	31					

MONDAY 3

MENU:

TUESDAY 4

MENU:

WEDNESDAY 5

MENU:

THURSDAY 6

MENU:

FRIDAY 7

MENU:

SATURDAY 8

SUNDAY 9

MENU:

MENU:

TASKS LIST

December 10 » December 16

Let the heavens rejoice, and let
the earth be glad; let the sea roar,
and the fulness thereof.

PSALM 96:11

							1
DECEMBER	2	3	4	5	6	7	8
	9	10	11	12	13	14	15
	16	17	18	19	20	21	22
	23	24	25	26	27	28	29
	30	31					

MONDAY 10

MENU:

TUESDAY 11

MENU:

cut here

WEDNESDAY 12

MENU:

THURSDAY 13

MENU:

FRIDAY 14

MENU:

SATURDAY 15

SUNDAY 16

MENU:

MENU:

TASKS LIST

December 17 » December 23

_____   _____

_____   _____

_____   _____

_____   _____

_____   _____

_____   _____

_____   _____

Serve the LORD with gladness:
come before his presence with singing.
PSALM 100:2

DECEMBER						1
2	3	4	5	6	7	8
9	10	11	12	13	14	15
16	17	18	19	20	21	22
23	24	25	26	27	28	29
30	31					

MONDAY 17

MENU:

TUESDAY 18

MENU:

WEDNESDAY 19

MENU:

THURSDAY 20

MENU:

FRIDAY 21

MENU:

SATURDAY 22

SUNDAY 23

MENU:

MENU:

TASKS LIST

When they saw the star, they rejoiced with exceeding great joy. And when they were come into the house, they saw the young child with Mary his mother, and fell down, and worshipped him.

MATTHEW 2:10, 11

DECEMBER							1
	2	3	4	5	6	7	8
	9	10	11	12	13	14	15
	16	17	18	19	20	21	22
	23	24	25	26	27	28	29
	30	31					

MONDAY 24

CHRISTMAS EVE

MENU:

TUESDAY 25

CHRISTMAS DAY

MENU:

cut here

WEDNESDAY 26

MENU:

THURSDAY 27

MENU:

FRIDAY 28

MENU:

SATURDAY 29

SUNDAY 30

MENU:

MENU:

TASKS LIST

_____ _____
_____ _____
_____ _____
_____ _____
_____ _____
_____ _____
_____ _____
_____ _____
_____ _____

While I live will I praise the LORD:
I will sing praises unto my God
while I have any being.
PSALM 146:2

JANUARY						
	31	1	2	3	4	5
	6	7	8	9	10	11	12
	13	14	15	16	17	18	19
	20	21	22	23	24	25	26
	27	28	29	30	31		

MONDAY 31

NEW YEAR'S EVE

MENU:

TUESDAY 1

NEW YEAR'S DAY

MENU:

cut here

WEDNESDAY 2

MENU:

THURSDAY 3

MENU:

FRIDAY 4

MENU:

SATURDAY 5

SUNDAY 6

MENU:

MENU:

NOTES

TASKS LIST

T A S K S   L I S T

TASKS LIST

TASKS LIST

TASKS LIST

NOTES

_____

PROJECTS + EVENTS

PROJECTS + EVENTS

PROJECTS + EVENTS

PROJECTS + EVENTS

_____

_____

PROJECTS + EVENTS

PROJECTS + EVENTS

_____

_____

PROJECTS + EVENTS

PROJECTS + EVENTS

PROJECTS + EVENTS

PROJECTS + EVENTS

PROJECTS + EVENTS

PROJECTS + EVENTS

PROJECTS + EVENTS

NOTES

NAME	NUMBER	ADDRESS

INFORMATION

NAME	NUMBER	ADDRESS

INFORMATION

NAME	NUMBER	ADDRESS

INFORMATION

NAME	NUMBER	ADDRESS

INFORMATION

NAME	NUMBER	ADDRESS

INFORMATION

NAME	NUMBER	ADDRESS

INFORMATION

NAME	NUMBER	ADDRESS

INFORMATION

NOTES

SHOPPING
LIST

SHOPPING
LIST

SHOPPING
LIST

SHOPPING
LIST

SHOPPING
LIST

SHOPPING
LIST

SHOPPING **LIST**

SHOPPING **LIST**

SHOPPING **LIST**

SHOPPING **LIST**

SHOPPING **LIST**

SHOPPING **LIST**

SHOPPING
LIST

SHOPPING
LIST

SHOPPING
LIST

SHOPPING
LIST

SHOPPING
LIST

SHOPPING
LIST

SHOPPING
LIST

SHOPPING
LIST

SHOPPING
LIST

SHOPPING
LIST

SHOPPING
LIST

SHOPPING
LIST

SHOPPING
LIST

SHOPPING
LIST

SHOPPING
LIST

SHOPPING
LIST

SHOPPING
LIST

SHOPPING
LIST

SHOPPING
LIST

SHOPPING
LIST

SHOPPING
LIST

SHOPPING
LIST

SHOPPING
LIST

SHOPPING
LIST

SHOPPING
LIST

SHOPPING
LIST

SHOPPING
LIST

SHOPPING
LIST

SHOPPING
LIST

SHOPPING
LIST

SHOPPING
LIST

SHOPPING
LIST

SHOPPING
LIST

SHOPPING
LIST

SHOPPING
LIST

SHOPPING
LIST

SHOPPING
LIST

SHOPPING
LIST

SHOPPING
LIST

SHOPPING **LIST**

SHOPPING **LIST**

SHOPPING **LIST**

SHOPPING
LIST

SHOPPING
LIST

SHOPPING
LIST

SHOPPING
LIST

SHOPPING
LIST

SHOPPING
LIST

SHOPPING
LIST

SHOPPING
LIST

SHOPPING
LIST

SHOPPING
LIST

SHOPPING
LIST

SHOPPING
LIST

SHOPPING
LIST

SHOPPING
LIST

SHOPPING
LIST

SHOPPING
LIST

SHOPPING
LIST

SHOPPING
LIST

SHOPPING **LIST**

SHOPPING **LIST**

SHOPPING **LIST**

SHOPPING
LIST

SHOPPING
LIST

SHOPPING
LIST

SHOPPING
LIST

SHOPPING
LIST

SHOPPING
LIST

SHOPPING
LIST

SHOPPING
LIST

SHOPPING
LIST

SHOPPING
LIST

SHOPPING
LIST

SHOPPING
LIST

SHOPPING
LIST

SHOPPING
LIST

SHOPPING
LIST

SHOPPING
LIST

SHOPPING
LIST

SHOPPING
LIST

SHOPPING LIST

SHOPPING LIST

SHOPPING LIST

SHOPPING **LIST**

SHOPPING **LIST**

SHOPPING **LIST**

SHOPPING **LIST**

SHOPPING **LIST**

SHOPPING **LIST**

CLOTHING SIZES

CLOTHING SIZES

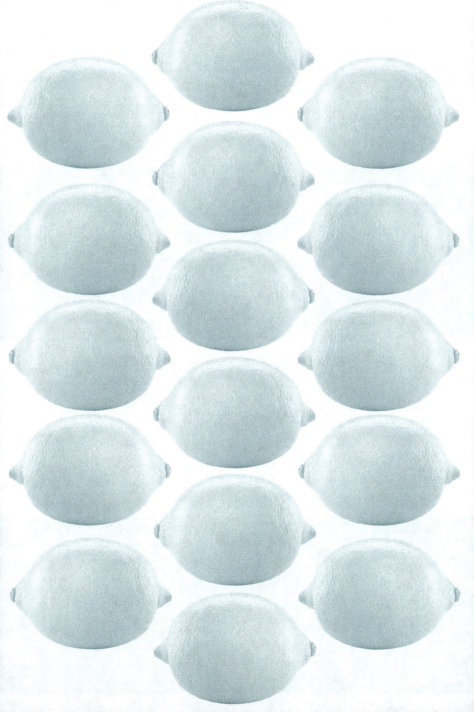

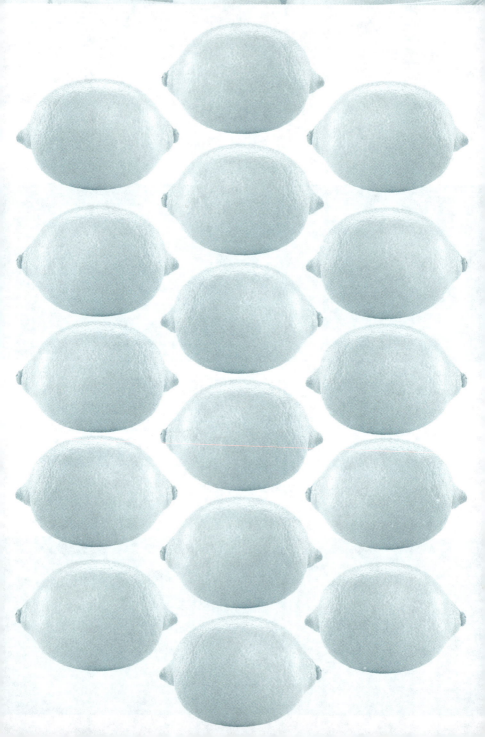

MASTER SHOPPING LIST

FRUIT	MEAT	BAKING	BREAKFAST
			PASTA + RICE
VEGETABLES	FROZEN		
		MISCELLANEOUS	BAKERY

MASTER SHOPPING LIST

PERSONAL CARE	CLEANING	SEASONINGS	CANS + JARS

	PAPER PRODUCTS	SAUCES + CONDIMENTS	REFRIGERATED

MEDICATIONS	DRINKS	CHILDCARE	
			ANIMALS

MASTER SHOPPING LIST

FRUIT	MEAT	BAKING	BREAKFAST

PASTA + RICE

VEGETABLES	FROZEN		

		MISCELLANEOUS	BAKERY

MASTER SHOPPING LIST

PERSONAL CARE	CLEANING	SEASONINGS	CANS + JARS
	PAPER PRODUCTS	SAUCES + CONDIMENTS	REFRIGERATED
MEDICATIONS	DRINKS	CHILDCARE	
			ANIMALS

CHECKLIST FOR _____

CHECKLIST FOR _____

CHECKLIST FOR _____

CHECKLIST FOR _____

_____ _____ _____ _____
_____ _____ _____ _____
_____ _____ _____ _____
_____ _____ _____ _____
_____ _____ _____ _____
_____ _____ _____ _____

CHECKLIST FOR _____

_____ _____ _____ _____
_____ _____ _____ _____
_____ _____ _____ _____
_____ _____ _____ _____
_____ _____ _____ _____
_____ _____ _____ _____

CHECKLIST FOR _____

_____ _____ _____ _____
_____ _____ _____ _____
_____ _____ _____ _____
_____ _____ _____ _____
_____ _____ _____ _____

ORDER FORM

To order, send this completed order form to:

CHRISTIAN LIGHT PUBLICATIONS

P.O. Box 1212 . Harrisonburg, VA 22803-1212

Phone: 1-800-776-0478 · 540-434-1003 · 8:30-5:00 EST

Fax: 540-433-8896 · E-mail: orders@clp.org · Web: www.clp.org

_____ _____
Name   Date

_____ _____
Mailing Address   Phone

_____
City   State   Zip

2018 Daily Planner   Qty. _____ x $14.99 ea. = _____

2019 Daily Planner   Qty. _____ x $14.99 ea. = _____

(Prices subject to change without notice)

Order Summary

☐ Check here to receive our free catalog of storybooks, activity books, tracts and more.

Order Subtotal _____ A

5.3% VA Tax (based on A)
(VA residents only) + _____ B

Shipping
• Orders up to $44.50 add $4.00
• Orders $44.51 and over add 9% of A + _____ C

TOTAL of A, B & C _____

All Payments in US Dollars

☐ Check/Money Order   ☐ Visa

☐ MasterCard   ☐ Discover   ☐ American Express

Name on Card _____

_____ - _____ - _____ - _____
Charge Card Number

_____ _____
Exp. Date   Signature

*For orders shipping outside the U.S.
please call the order department or order online at www.clp.org*

THANK YOU FOR YOUR ORDER!

THANK YOU
FOR CHOOSING
the

20 18 | HOMEMAKER'S FRIEND
DAILY PLANNER